The Manager's Pocket Guide to Preventing Sexual Harassment

Terry L. Fitzwater

HRD Press • Amherst • Massachusetts

Publisher and/or author make no warranties, express or implied, with respect to this book and neither assumes any responsibility for any legal complaint or action occasioned by following its guidelines. The user assumes all risk and liability whatsoever in connection with the use of or reliance upon the materials contained herein and there are no oral agreements or understandings or warranties collateral to or affecting the understanding implicit in the purchase of this book.

Mr. Fitzwater's book is not intended to provide legal advice, and it should not be viewed as a substitute for obtaining legal advice. You should always contact an attorney familiar with employment law to ascertain the lawfulness and legal ramifications of disciplinary actions.

©1998 by Terry Fitzwater

Published by:

HRD Press
22 Amherst Road
Amherst, MA 01002
1-800-822-2801 (U.S. and Canada)
413-253-3488
413-253-3490 (FAX)
www.hrdpress.com

ISBN 0-87425-450-7

Cover design by Eileen Klockars
Editorial services by Suzanne Bay
Production services by Clark Riley

Printed in Canada

CONTENTS

PREFACE

THIS GUIDEBOOK is dedicated to every manager who has had the unfortunate experience of hearing the words, "I've been harassed." In today's litigious business society, these three words are probably enough to send shivers down your spine. The resultant crosscurrent of misinformation that ultimately flows throughout the organization, despite your best efforts to keep this type of complaint confidential, can negatively impact the company and its employees for months. Who is ultimately hurt? Everyone.

Is harassment really an issue today, or has it quieted down over the last several years? Pick up any newspaper and you will see that it's still a newsworthy, albeit discomforting issue. Further proof of its persistence as a workplace problem can be found in a study conducted in 1997 by a major labor organization. The study asked a number of business women if sexual harassment is still an issue. An incredible 78% answered in the affirmative. And in 1998, a new twist was addressed by the Supreme Court of the United States: same sex harassment. Writing for the court, Justice Antonin Scalia said, to paraphrase,

". . . it is not . . . gender nor sexual orientation that matters. Only the harasser's conduct, not his or her desire, matters." Justice Scalia opined that sexual discrimination that threatened one's ability to work is egregious, especially if the behavior is "so objectively offensive" as to "create an environment that a reasonable person would find hostile or abusive."

Workplace harassment is alarming for both the employer and his or her employees. Unfortunately, studies conducted by the Equal Employment Opportunity Commission show that it is also a disturbing trend.

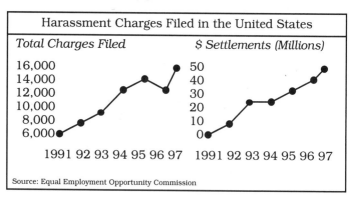

Harassment Charges Filed in the United States

Total Charges Filed

$ Settlements (Millions)

Source: Equal Employment Opportunity Commission

In 1991, 6,883 harassment charges were filed in the United States, resulting in $7.1 million in settlement costs. These numbers increased to 15,889 charges and $49.5 million in settlement costs by 1997. A new "industry" was created as a result: providing harassment liability insurance to cover the costs of these suits. But is this the answer? I would challenge that it is a short-term solution, at best. It never gets to the issue of prevention.

Recent Court Decision

The issue of sexual harassment has been troublesome for employers in another way: Its message has been somewhat "cloudy." the Supreme Court has finally added language to help clarify some of the finer points of confusion. In a June 1998 decision, Justices Kennedy and Souter wrote:

> *"An employer is subject to vicarious liability to a victimized employee for an actionable hostile environment created by a supervisor with immediate (or successively higher) authority over the employee." And, "When no tangible employment action is taken, a defending employer may raise an affirmative defense to liability or damages, subject to proof by a preponderance of the evidence."*

What does this mean?

❏ An employee refusing to submit to a manager's sexual advances can sue the company even if the manager did not follow through on threats to make the employee's work life intolerable.

But,

❏ The employer can help defend itself, and may be relieved of liability in the absence of tangible harm, by showing it had a sexual harassment policy, it communicated it to its employees, it provided a means to report harassment, the company reacted promptly to the harasser's behavior, and the complaining employee "unreasonably failed" to report the problem through proper company channels.

This is good news, bad news. Good if you monitor the work place actions of your employees, bad if you don't. But let's take a step back for a moment. Could you or the company have prevented the alleged harassment? Perhaps not. But its likelihood could have been lessened if the company had not ignored it in the first place. There is an old saying, "Ignoring it won't make it go away." This couldn't be more true in the case of workplace harassment. This is how you deal with harassment: You hit it head-on, through education. Remember this:

> *The more the issue is brought to light, the greater the chances of reducing its occurrence.*

I have had discussions with some who disagree with my last statement. They sincerely believe that if you teach what harassment is, you only increase the likelihood of someone filing a discrimination charge or a lawsuit. In effect, their view is that information is power. I take the opposite approach: I believe it is misinformation that supplies power, while correct information creates understanding.

So, we are back to this guide. What it will provide is a methodology and a process to deal with misinformation and eliminate as much of it as possible.

INTRODUCTION

HARASSMENT. The mere thought of it is enough to send anyone into a panic, especially if you are named as the alleged harasser. How about Clarence Thomas? Would you be comfortable in his shoes? My guess is that you would not be. Consider the following conversation shared with me when I worked in the area of human resources:

Employee:	Terry, I need to share something with you.
Me:	*You look troubled.*
Employee:	I am. Something has happened today and I don't know how to deal with it. I've told the person to stop. But he hasn't.
Me:	*You told the person to stop what?*
Employee:	Asking me out on a date. I've told him I want ours to be a professional relationship. I have no desire to see him socially.
Me:	*How many times have you told him this?*
Employee:	Several. Now he has called me at home. This is way out of control.
Me:	*Let's talk.*

I hope this is a conversation you never have to face yourself. But if some of this sounds all too familiar, this book can help. It will help to answer this question: *What is the best I can do to make sure the workplace is free from harassment and that all employees enjoy a professional working environment?*

This is a lofty goal. This guidebook, however, will help you establish such a culture and help minimize the chances of multimillion dollar harassment suits. In these suits, ignorance is not bliss: if you stand on ground labeled "I didn't know," the surface will quickly turn into quicksand.

THE PURPOSE OF THIS GUIDEBOOK

My intention with this book is twofold:

(1) To take a close look at what harassment is and (just as important) to examine what it is not.
(2) To equip leaders and employees with a methodology to stop harassment before it starts.

This material will also help you establish the following:

- The development of a culture sensitive to the needs of the individual.

- A climate of understanding about diversity in the workplace.

- A methodology for investigating alleged claims of harassment and how to deal with the information.

- Policies to inform and educate.

HOW TO USE THIS GUIDEBOOK

This book follows a natural course of events. It is essential that you read each chapter before you go on to the next. If you skip to a specific section, it might confuse you because you do not have the benefit of the knowledge from earlier chapters. *Do not skip ahead.*

Keep in mind the purpose of this book as you read it. It is a road map to recognition and prevention. It is intended to offer suggestions about how to reinforce a strong employee-oriented culture or begin a process leading to positive cultural change. It is ultimately about respect for the individual, for differences in gender, ethnicity, backgrounds, and even philosophies.

> *Harassment prevention is about respect*

Changing your workplace culture will be difficult unless everyone understands, or at least tolerates, a person's right to his or her differences and opinions. All organizations that are serious about harassment prevention need to shine a spotlight on those differences, rather than hide them. How do you do that effectively? Let's look at the following:

The Five A's of Understanding

This simple formula will assist you in creating an environment that is accepting or tolerant of differences and free from harassment.

- ❑ **A**ppreciate and celebrate workforce diversity.

- ❑ **A**dvance the understanding of different cultures and ideologies.

- ❑ **A**lways tune in to the messages sent to you.

- ❑ **A**nnounce at every opportunity your commitment to create a professional work environment free of unacceptable behaviors.

- ❑ **A**lign your policies and procedures to reflect your attitude and statements.

We will look at some ways to make the 5 A's a reality at the end of the book.

THE EMPLOYER AUDIT TO ASSESS LIABILITY

An important preliminary to using the guidebook is the completion of the "Employer Audit to Assess Liability." A "no" answer to any of the questions is a signal that you should investigate the organization's current methodology for dealing with the issue in question. Let's take a look.

WORKSHEET		
EMPLOYER AUDIT TO ASSESS LIABILITY		

DIRECTIONS: *Read the following questions and check off your answers. A "no" response signals the need for you to investigate company methods.*

	Question	Yes	No
(1)	Do you have a harassment prevention policy?		
(2)	Is the policy disseminated at hire?		
(3)	Is the policy posted where all can read it?		
(4)	Is there a mechanism to address employee concerns/complaints on harassment?		
(5)	Are employees trained in harassment, its prevention, and the company's policy of zero-tolerance?		

(continued)

	Question	**Yes**	**No**
(6)	Do employees sign an attendance sheet recording participation in training?		
(7)	Does the harassment policy state...?		
	• Harassment is not tolerated by the company		
	• Harassment is against the law		
	• Retaliation is prohibited		
	• How to file a complaint and report harassment		
	• The definitions of harassment		
(8)	Do you supply vendors who visit your property with a copy of your harassment policy?		

If you answered yes to all of these questions, congratulations. You have taken affirmative steps that will reap dividends if you ever find yourself faced with the kind of employee situation I described. There is also a second benefit. A harassment policy in place suggests that you are taking a proactive approach to this issue. This will help you defend your company's actions in court if:

(1) you terminated someone for their actions and he or she is suing for wrongful termination, or

(2) the charging party is suing, claiming you did nothing to prevent the action.

Proactive versus reactive won't necessarily win your case, but it will demonstrate *intent to prevent*. Any information you can supply to establish *intent to prevent* can create the doubt you need to increase your chances of winning.

If you answered "no" to any of the questions, you need to resolve the issue. For instance, if you answered "no" to *Do you have a sexual harassment policy?* then you need to develop one. I have included a model at the end of this book that should be of help. Here is a brief statement found in most employee handbooks as an introduction:

Our Philosophy

Sexual harassment is prohibited by our company and by law. It is our intent to provide all employees with a workplace free of harassment or inappropriate activity related to sex, race, religion, age, ethnic or national origin, disability, sexual preference, or personal characteristic.

Does any of this sound familiar? It should, since it is a basic non-discrimination statement with sexual harassment added. This makes it a basic tenet in the work arena today, important to adopt for reasons of legality, morality, and for employee morale.

All "no" answers need to be researched. I suggest you assign a team to:

(1) Research how you currently handle the item in question.

(2) Make recommendations for compliance.

Harassment. We now understand that it is more than just a term to fear. Its definition has been broadened to include the need to understand varying cultures and to value the diversity that each individual brings to the workplace. Let's take a closer look at the term in order to increase our current awareness.

1
THE BASICS OF HARASSMENT

What Is Harassment? To understand
harassment, you need to know what it is as well
as what it is not. Webster's *New World Dictionary*
(Second College Edition) defines it as:

(1) *Trouble* persistently
(2) *Discrimination* on the *basis of sex*
(3) To trouble, *worry,* or *torment*

This sounds too simple, and the italicized words
only reinforce the simplicity by sounding quite
threatening. However, in the "real world," what
constitutes harassment is confusing and
peppered with gray areas. We will take a test in a
moment, but first let's see how you view yourself
and your knowledge of the issues involving
harassment.

The Harassment Awareness Grid		
	And	
	I can define them	I can't define them
I'm aware of most of the principles attributable to the issue of harassment	+	−
I'm aware of some of the principles attributable to the issue of harassment	−	−

Problematic

If you place yourself in any square designated by a minus (-) sign, this is a problem you must address. The term "harassment" has too many interpretations for you to be comfortable with any understanding less than positive (+).

To get a better understanding, and to see if your self-assessment is accurate, let's take a test.

IS IT HARASSMENT?

Read the following questions and indicate whether or not you think the situation or statement involves harassment.

1. John and Mary have dinner after work one day. John starts to call repeatedly and occasionally writes Mary notes. She wants nothing to do with him socially, is upset by his actions, and has told him so.

2. Continued bothersome and annoying conduct is not harassment.

3. A single unexpected flirtation is harassment.

4. A single accidental touch or some other kind of accidental physical contact can be harassment.

5. Commenting on how sexy someone looks is sexual harassment.

6. Looking at a co-worker isn't harassment. Constantly staring at them can be harassment.

7. Unwanted and unwelcome conduct is included in the definition of harassment.

8. Interviewing someone in a hotel room is harassment.

9. Telling ethnic, off-color, or dirty jokes to a co-worker is harassment.

10. A person overhearing such a joke and is offended can claim harassment.

11. A calendar of muscle men hanging in a woman's office or cubicle constitutes harassment.

12. Asking a co-worker out on a date is harassment.

13. Telling a person his/her hair looks nice is harassment.

Yes (1,2,6,7,10)

If you did not score well, don't be too concerned at this point. The purpose of this guide is to help you identify the gray areas. To understand why numbers 3, 4, 8, 9, 11, 12, and 13 are not considered harassment, you need to be aware of what harassment *is* and *is not*. You can understand the reasons if you look closely at the questions. We will take them one at a time.

Question #3:   This is not harassment because it is a *single* flirtatious episode. The word "single" is important. The law does not eliminate sexuality from the workplace. It cannot be done. If someone flirts, the other person says "no," the word is taken at its face value, and the flirting is stopped, *there is no harassment.* Likewise, if the flirtation is not flagrant and if the behavior ceases when it is brought to the person's attention, it is not harassment.

> *The law will not eliminate sexuality from the workplace.*

Question #4:   The key word here is *accidental.* The thing to do is apologize and move on.

14

Question #8: Interviewing someone in a hotel room is questionable conduct, but it is not harassment. If you find yourself in this situation, leave the door open.

Question #9: If two people tell each other jokes of questionable workplace value and they both welcome the jokes, it is not harassment.

Question #12: Asking a person out on a date is not harassment. It becomes harassment if the person says no and the activity continues.

Question # 13: Complimenting someone is not harassment unless the person objects to it or the comments cross the line and become more personal.

Some of these questions raise another important issue pertaining to the definition of harassment:

> *Know your audience*

This simply means that what may be offensive to one person might not be to another. For example, if the two people telling the off-color joke in question #9 welcome the joke, it is not harassment. But if they are approached by a third party, the joke telling stops, *especially if they know the new person will find it offensive.* To reiterate, if they do not know the person's predisposition to offensive jokes, the joke telling stops.

Knowing your audience also comes into play in questions #5 and #11. If the sexy comment or the calendar is welcomed, there is no harassment. But one should always avoid anything that compromises a professional working environment, and these examples certainly come close to crossing the line. We will explore this whole area in more detail later, as we expand our discussion on the issue of harassment.

DIVERSITY

Any discussion of harassment must include the topic of diversity. It is defined in the *New World Dictionary* as follows:

(1) Quality, state, fact or instance of being diverse; differences

The French have a nice way of sounding the horn on the issue of diversity with the phrase "Vive le difference."

A number of considerations surface as you delve deeper into the meaning. Factors such as one's culture, heritage, or experiences each uniquely shape an individual and how he or she perceives and even reacts to differing situations and issues. I was raised in the South and grew up with two stereotypes that, to this day, I wrestle with constantly: people from the South are all bigots and do not rate high on the intelligence scale. So what's the point? If you knew that these unfair stereotypes irritated me, would you approach me any differently? If you knew an African American resented the word "boy" because of its negative associations, would you avoid using the phrase? I think so. Here's a paraphrase to remember:

> *Absolute understanding increases understanding absolutely.*

In other words, if we are cognizant of a person's predispositions, we can and should alter our behavior to avoid misunderstandings.

ASSESSING YOUR DIVERSITY CLIMATE: A SURVEY

To discover if your organization is perceived as one that embraces the concept of diversity, ask your employees these simple questions:

Diversity Management Questions
1. How would you describe the work climate? Is it supportive? Why or why not?
2. How has the company contributed to your personal growth through an understanding of your needs?
3. What do you like best about working here?
4. What do you like least about working here?
5. Do you think your co-workers and the company understand your culture and heritage?
6. Do you feel that opportunity exists here for everyone, regardless of color or gender? Why or why not?
7. What is the image of women, men, or people of color here?
8. Do you feel free to discuss any issue with anyone you desire?

That's it. Eight questions to enlightenment. The responses could be eye-openers. A word of caution, however: anytime you survey, you set up the expectation that *something will be done* concerning the answers. If you are not prepared to deal with the responses, don't administer the survey.

As an example of responses, I administered this survey to a group of technicians at a computer manufacturing facility. The findings were frank and diverse. Here are some comments:

"There are two manufacturing sites here. The people at the other site look down on us because we are hourly workers."

"Women and people of color must make a conscious effort to fit here; otherwise, we go unnoticed."

The company referred to in these examples held sensitivity sessions to explore the comments further. They empowered the people to make recommendations on ways to improve. This is a good beginning.

Empowerment creates ownership

VALUE SYSTEMS

As I said, the understanding of others begins only after we understand and take a close look at ourselves. What we are and what we say and do are based on our experiences and exposures. Let's look at the following:

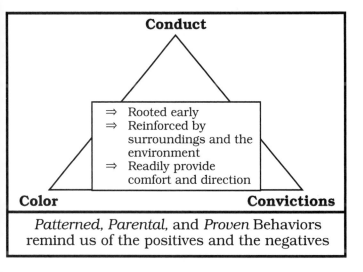

The chart is not as complicated as it appears. Let's add clarity through definition.

The **Conduct** we display is evidenced in the various situations in which we are placed.

• At a rock concert I may stand and sing. Where I work I wouldn't think of letting anyone see that side of me.

We tend to **Color** things based on the ideas, ideals, and biases developed in each of us as a result of our culture, our geographical environment, and our teachings.

• He is from the South, so he must be a bigot and not very smart.

Our **Convictions** are the "actuals."
• If we see a rock, we call it a rock.

All three have in common the fact that they are patterned, parental, and proven.

Patterned Behavior

Patterned behavior is "mirrored." That is, a person will tend to emulate the behavior of someone they respect or admire.

Parental Behavior

Parental behavior is copied. If a parent is college educated, the son or daughter is more likely to want to go to college. If the parent is a strong disciplinarian, chances are that the child will display the same attribute later in life.

Proven Behavior

Proven behavior develops from the college of hard knocks. If I touch a hot stove, I know I will get burned.

These behaviors have three things in common:

(1) *They take **root** early in our lives* . Our formative years are generally birth to the mid-teens.

(2) They are continually **reinforced** by the environment and our surroundings, where we grow up, what we see others do, and how they react.

(3) *They* **readily** *provide comfort.* We tend to fall back on those things that are comfortable to us.

In each type of behavior, there is both positive and negative. I'll use myself as an example. First, my Positive relates to the sixties. I have great memories of that time period. High school was fun. The Motown sound had just burst onto the scene. To this day, when I hear a Motown song on the radio, I have to crank up the volume; it reminds me of an enjoyable time in my life. Vietnam does not. It is my Negative.

This brings us to the point of this review.

> *The only constant is change*

We cannot change, we will not change, unless we recognize and deal with our own biases.

Identifying Bias & Behavior Exercise

Ask yourself the following questions and record your answers. Be honest with your responses.

(1) Do I treat everyone as I would like to be treated?

(2) Do I look at those I work with, regardless of race or gender, as learned business associates instead of as objects of my biases?

(3) Do I take the time to understand the individual needs of my associates?

If the answer is "no" or even a qualified "maybe," develop your action plan by asking yourself, *What am I going to do about it?* Get others to help you. Ask for their feedback. You should go no further in this book until you have challenged *your* perceptions.

WHAT HARASSMENT PREVENTION IS

Harassment and diversity go hand in hand. To eliminate harassment, you need to increase cultural and social awareness within your organization by coming to terms with your biases, beliefs, and behaviors. This should be understood, eventually, by every single person in your organization.

Preventing Harassment

We help prevent harassment when we:

- Understand differences

- Accept the uniqueness of others

- Know our audience

- Modify behaviors to the norms of the organization and society

- Understand and modify our biases, beliefs, behaviors

- Practice what we preach

Frankly, *use common sense.* Stop signs do not send a signal to slow down. As I once heard it said, *What part of no don't you understand? The "n" or the "o"?*

Before we move on, let's revisit *patterned behavior* for a moment. It can be a powerful tool used to your advantage. How? By setting examples within the organization. In other words, let your actions speak for you. If your actions display a positive attitude, then chances are your employees will also approach the day with a positive outlook. If your attitude is one that helps others, chances are good that a helping hand will be offered by others.

> *Positive displays yield positive results.*

Harassment, as you can see from this review, is a complex issue. To understand it better we will expand its meaning in the next chapter by looking at additional definitions.

2
HARASSMENT: MOVING BEYOND THE BASICS

Origins

The ideal of creating a workplace free from harassment took some time to develop. It was not that long ago when the concept of harassment (and, in fact, its very definition) was foreign to the work environment. Workers who were made uncomfortable by the ignorance and behavior of others sparked a change in attitude. It was our judicial system that supplied the impetus, when the first harassment lawsuit hit the business community. Workplace philosophies clearly needed to be changed significantly.

Attitude Adjustment	
1960's and 1970's *Attitude*	**1980's and beyond** *Replaced with*
• Policies to inform and **regulate**..................	Policies to inform and **prevent**
• **Reactive** to issues...........	**Proactive** to issues
• **Ignorance** is bliss...........	**Awareness** is a must
• Personal **relationships** don't matter.....................	Keep it **professional**

It was no longer enough to expect self-regulation. Policies to protect rather than to regulate were drafted and implemented. A new attitude appeared, evidenced by this handbook language:

> *We expect all of our employees to conduct themselves with professionalism at all times and in all situations. Any conduct deemed inappropriate in the workplace will be immediately brought to the employee's attention for correction.*

A process to deal with less than professional behaviors will be presented in a later chapter.

WHAT IS HARASSMENT?

The definition of harassment has broadened over time. It originally referred almost exclusively to the male/female relationship, but grew to include the issue of same-sex harassment, and hostile working environment. A hostile work environment is defined as working conditions so intolerable that they create extreme stress in employees. (The employee who voluntarily quits as a result has an actionable case based on the concept of constructive discharge.)

Let's take a closer look at this by drawing a minor distinction between workplace harassment and sexual harassment. These two concepts will be presented in a format suitable for inclusion in an employee handbook or a policy and procedures manual, and should be posted on all bulletin boards.

Workplace Harassment: A Definition

Workplace harassment is any *unwelcome* or *unwanted* conduct based on an individual's race, sex, disability, sexual preference, ethnic origin, age, religion, or other personal characteristic.

You will notice the inclusion once again of the term *sexual preference*. In most states, this is a policy option. In states such as California, it is the law. The winds of change are blowing and if it is not currently required in your state, it is likely to be in the not-too-distant future. You may want to consider its adoption and beat the rush. At the very least, you will want to consult the labor code in your state for specifics.

Sexual Harassment: Defined

Sexual harassment is a form of sex discrimination that involves unwanted or unwelcome conduct. Most cases involve and allege that a male has harassed a female. Harassment may also involve persons of the same sex or female to male. Sexual harassment is further defined as any unwanted or unwelcome verbal, non-verbal, or physical advance, request for sexual favors, or other conduct of a sexual nature that affects an individual's work environment.

You will note that our definition now includes any verbal, non-verbal, or physical advance and any request for sexual favors. In the case of verbal or physical advances or a request for sexual favors, the law is fairly clear. These can be objectively measured: the alleged harasser has either said something or has not. He or she has acted physically or has not. The real difficulty comes from the subjective area of non-verbal harassment. Let's explore each of the sub-areas for clarification.

Verbal, Physical, or Non-Verbal Harassment

Verbal harassment includes racial or ethnic slurs; sexual innuendo or other suggestive comments; humor and jokes about sex, race, religion, disability, age, or gender-specific traits; sexual advances or propositions; insults and threats.

This is quite a laundry list, and it was intended as such when it was written. The fact that it is so encompassing sends us a strong message: to *think* before saying anything that might be misconstrued by the receiving party. Look closely at the list. Is there anything that doesn't make sense?

A point of clarification. I'm often asked for an example of sexual innuendo. A good example presented itself while I was boarding a major airline carrier. A number of passengers were trying to board as a male mechanic was trying to deplane. It was quite a task for him. Someone in our line said to him, "It looks like you are having a hard time getting off." His response in front of his female partner, who was standing next to me, was, "Yeah, if I don't get off at least once a day, I don't feel right." Take it from me, his partner was not amused, nor the customers who heard the remark.

The act of **Physical** harassment virtually defines itself. It is the intentional touching of another's body (e.g., pinching, brushing, patting), kissing, the inappropriate display of a part of one's body, coerced acts of a sexual nature, or demeaning actions or activities (e.g., pushing, blocking a pathway) based on age, ethnicity, sex, or race.

The key word at work here is *intentional.* At one time or another most of us have turned around without looking and bumped a co-worker in an inappropriate way. This is not harassment, and one should extend his or her apology and walk away. A word of caution: intent is not an absolute defense. The company will need to investigate carefully to get at the facts. We will look at the investigative process in Chapter Four.

Some of the actions associated with **Non-Verbal** harassment are much more difficult to prove or disprove. It is defined as leering; whistling; suggestive or insulting looks, sounds, gestures, pictures, cartoons, or calendars; and the display or distribution of offensive or derogatory written materials.

And herein lies the problem. How *does* one leer? What *is* a suggestive look? What *is* an insulting look or sound? The law in this area is vague and somewhat undefined and it is very difficult to determine one person's intent versus another's perception. Here is something to remember:

> *Perception is reality.*

And it *is* reality each and every time. If this is a basic premise, it signals the use of an investigative process to get at the truth. We will take a look at this subject later. For now, remember that you *must* investigate.

One other note. The advent of e-mail has made it easy to distribute sexually explicit material. I strongly suggest a policy with sanctions for improper use of this media as follows:

> The distribution of any electronic mail material deemed harassing in nature is strictly prohibited. Any person found in violation of this policy will be subject to discipline up to and including termination."

Four Questions to Clarity

Let's take a different approach in our definition of harassment by asking ourselves the following concerning an alleged event:

Is It Harassment?
(1) Did the behavior of the accused create an intimidating, offensive, or hostile working environment?
(2) Did the behavior signal to the charging party a condition of employment, or was it used as the basis of any employment decision?
(3) Was the behavior unwelcome or unwanted?
(4) Did the behavior substantially interfere with the employee's work performance?

A "yes" answer to any of these questions will also signal the need for an investigation. You should note that the questions come directly from our earlier explanations of harassment. The words should by now sound very familiar. For further clarity, let's look at them one at a time.

(1) Did the alleged behavior of the accused create an intimidating, offensive, or hostile working environment?

In this case, always keep in mind that it is the perception of the harassed and not the intent of the harasser that matters. As an example, the harasser may view his or her use of off-color language as perfectly acceptable. If it has gone unchallenged or has never been brought to his or her attention, how would the harasser know it is unacceptable?

(2) Did the behavior signal to the charging party a condition of employment, or was it used as the basis for any employment decision?

A manager decides not to promote a female in his or her department because she has refused a date or the promotion of an employee is not supported by a boss because the person refused his or her advances. (What part of "no" don't you understand?)

(3) Did the behavior substantially interfere with the employee's work performance?

This is where the nature of the alleged event is considered so egregious that the person being harassed cannot comfortably perform his or her job. An example of this is when a manager continually and publicly chides one of his or her employees in front of others (e.g. with slurs) to the point of total embarrassment. Another example of such harassment is when a supervisor continually asks an employee for a date.

QUID PRO QUO

No discussion of the definitions of harassment should ignore the concept of quid pro quo. It means "something for something" or "this for that." Quid Pro Quo is always the example you see in sexual harassment training seminars: it is the one where the male is hanging over the female co-worker's desk, getting far too close to her for comfort. Another example is the television commercial with dialogue that goes something like this:

"You know, with a body like yours, you could really go places around here. Do you know what I mean?"

"Yes. I do know what you mean and this is harassment, and *I don't* have to take it."

In both examples the "something for something" that is presented is close to innuendo. You must read between the lines. Was it really harassment? Or was it misinterpreted by the receiver? *It doesn't matter!* Remember, perception *is* reality each and every time. In both of these examples, the harasser will need to explain his or her behavior to the investigator of the alleged event.

LANGUAGE USAGE

Sexual harassment is a serious charge to make against someone. In this country we are all innocent until proven guilty, but this is sometimes not the case when one is charged with sexual harassment. There seems to be a pattern of rushing to judgment. Be careful! Take your time to examine all of the issues and let the facts take you to a calculated, well-thought-out decision. Before drawing any conclusion, always use (as I have done so far in this book) the word *alleged*. It is important that you not damage the reputation of the alleged harasser. The accusation alone may harm the person, so do not add to the problem. You do not want the accused to seek legal redress against the company because of your statements, no matter how well intentioned you are.

Once you understand your own biases, you can begin to appreciate the differences in others and the diversity each brings to the workplace. Off-color jokes about a person's race won't seem as humorous. You might even find yourself leaving the scene because you don't see the purpose behind the joke other than to hurt. Does familiarity breed contempt? No. It breeds understanding and acceptance.

> *Familiarity leads to acceptance.*

The basics outlined here should help establish an understanding of harassment. Let's now examine a few basic rules designed to help you notify your employees of their rights and lessen the likelihood of lawsuits or charges of discrimination.

3
A FEW GROUND RULES

We will look at the investigation process in Chapter Four. Before we do, however, it is important that you understand a few basic ground rules. They are all based on one premise: *harassment* is a serious issue, and any alleged incident will be investigated. The company must act not only to protect the rights of the individual, but also to protect itself against litigation; harassment is, quite simply, *against the law.*

THE RULES

Notification Now

You must immediately notify all employees that harassment of any kind will not be tolerated. You can do so simply by placing the company's harassment policy in your policy and procedure manuals and handbooks, and posting it where all members of the organization can see it. It is also a good idea to distribute a position statement to all employees, old and new. It must include:

1. A statement of the company's commitment to prevent harassment
2. A definition of workplace harassment
3. A definition of sexual harassment
4. General conduct guidelines
5. Ways to stop harassment
6. Ways to report harassment

A sample policy is included at the end of this book.

Immediate Investigation

Each employee must be told that the company will investigate *any* report of harassment, as well as alleged improper conduct. It will do so in a timely manner, usually defined as *immediately*.

Quick action is important because recollections get hazy after a period of time and witnesses may begin to rationalize and make excuses for the alleged improper behavior. I saw this happen in a case where uninvited back rubbing became, "Well, I'm not sure. His hand was on her back, but maybe he was just patting her. Kind of a support thing." Time is an enemy to the truth, not an ally.

Confirm Confidentiality

Each person must be informed that the investigation will be conducted and in the strictest of confidence; the information uncovered will only be shared with those who *must know*. It is important at this point to inform any witness or person being interviewed that they must remain quiet about the issue. A statement I always use goes something like this:

> *You have been identified as someone with knowledge of the alleged events of January 3. "Jane" has stated that you witnessed them (or have knowledge of them). I need to ask you some questions to clarify what actually happened. Please note that we do not want to harm the reputation of either party, so I must ask you not to repeat what we discuss to anyone. Do you understand, and can I count on your discretion and confidence as it relates to this discussion?*

I have never had anyone take issue with this request. But let's suppose the person refuses to commit to your request for complete confidentiality. I recommend that you interview the party anyway. I would rather deal with the *possibility* of indiscretion than terminate someone without all of the facts.

Action is Assured

Each employee must know that there will be ramifications for any individual found to be in violation of the harassment prevention policy. The statement in your policy must include strong language such as:

"Any employee found in violation of our policy will be subject to appropriate corrective action, up to and including termination."

Rule of Retaliation

Occasionally, you will find that the alleged victim or the accused will seek some sort of retaliation. It might be subtle, or it might be blatant, but any retaliation becomes especially acute if one party works for the other. A supervisor cleared of wrongdoing can make it very difficult for the employee who made the complaint. You must state, in no uncertain terms, that this kind of retaliatory action will not be tolerated. Here is a typical policy statement that addresses this problem:

3. A Few Ground Rules

You will be advised of the results of the investigation. Retaliation against you or anyone who participates in the investigation will not be tolerated; the party who retaliates will be subject to disciplinary action up to and including termination for any unprofessional acts.

Let's summarize with a table:

Basic Rules for Harassment Investigation

Notification **N**ow
- ❑ Commitment to prevent
- ❑ Definition of workplace harassment
- ❑ Definition of sexual harassment
- ❑ General conduct guidelines
- ❑ Ways to stop harassment

Immediate **I**nvestigation
- ❑ Timely investigative process

Confirm **C**onfidentiality
- ❑ Those involved in the process are the only ones with a need to know.
- ❑ Interviewees are asked for secrecy.

Action is **A**ssured
- ❑ There is a penalty, up to and including termination, for improper conduct.

Rule of **R**etaliation
- ❑ Subtle or blatant acts of retaliation will not be tolerated.

3. A Few Ground Rules

I recommend that you follow each of these rules *to the letter* of their intent. They will show your employees that you are serious about preventing harassment. The rules will also:

(1) Demonstrate to outside parties (e.g., courts, arbitrators, juries) that your company is proactive in its approach to harassment prevention.

(2) A process has been implemented and it is followed.

(3) The process offers consistency of application.

(4) You have taken the necessary steps to ensure confidentiality.

(5) The rules allow for due process (procedural consistency) and a chance to respond to all allegations.

Of course, the key here is to *follow the rules* as you have written them. To do otherwise will alienate your employees when they interpret your policy as "for show" only. Any good attorney will point out that you failed to follow up and act on what you have established in writing.

It's now time to look at the investigation process.

4
THE INVESTIGATION PROCESS

The company must establish a mechanism to report alleged incidents of harassment. The use of an open door policy is a must when it comes to this issue. Every employee must feel comfortable that he or she can go to anyone in the organization to report his or her concerns. It is also a good idea to have a specific reporting process posted and included in the employee handbook. It will look like this:

Every employee should feel free to report any instance of harassment to any management official. It is always a good idea to report it first to your direct supervisor, as this individual has firsthand knowledge of the work area and its employees. If the alleged harasser is your supervisor, you should seek out your supervisor's supervisor. Human Resources is always available at any time to listen to your concerns.

THE FOUR C'S OF INVESTIGATION

The company has four goals in mind as it begins to investigate. It will:

(1) *Conduct* a confidential investigation.

(2) *Consult* with those who have knowledge of the alleged harassment.

(3) *Consider* the evidence in order to come to a rational and supported decision or conclusion.

(4) *Correct* through "affirmative action" any violation of the company's policy.

The investigation process begins with issue identification. That is, you must first determine if the issue is harassment before you proceed. In an earlier book, *The Manager's Pocket Guide to Documenting Employee Performance (HRD Press, 1998),* I developed a flowchart to demonstrate the process.

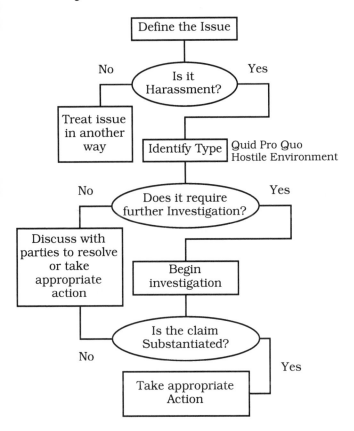

The chart offers four statements and three questions to assist in process fluency. The four statements are:

(1) Define the issue
(2) Identify the type
(3) Begin the investigation
(4) Take appropriate action

The chart asks three basic questions:

(1) Is it harassment?
(2) Does it require further investigation?
(3) Is the claim substantiated?

Each statement and question is designed to take you logically down a path toward a solution. Let's look at an example to see how it works.

Employee:	"I've been sexually harassed."
Me:	*"Would you explain what happened?*
Employee:	"My supervisor, John, said he would give me a raise if I was nice to him."
Me:	*"Did he define, 'nice to him'"?*
Employee:	"No. But I know what he meant."

For the sake of the example, let's leave it at this without further questioning.

The first thing that should pop into your head is something we raised earlier: the phrase *perception is reality*. This person thinks she was harassed. Therefore, to her way of thinking, it happened. This is enough to warrant an investigation or, at a minimum, enough to ask some questions.

Following the flowchart:

Define the issue: You need to determine the exact meaning behind "nice to him." It is reasonable to want to find out what the person meant by this stand-alone statement.

Is it harassment? You find through questioning that the answer is no. The alleged harasser claims that he was misunderstood, that he said he was "happy he could give her a raise and that it was nice of her to show her appreciation when he announced it to her." Others confirm that they didn't take his statement as derogatory or sexually motivated.

Action: Bring the two parties together to resolve or treat the issue in some other way. Face-to-face communication usually works the best.

If the answer is yes, however, identify the type. In this case you determine that it is sexual harassment, quid pro quo, because of the manager's statement *as verified by witnesses*, "Be nice and I will give you a raise."

Does it require further investigation? You determine through questioning that the answer is no. (The party may admit to the claim.) So, your action is to "discuss with the parties to resolve or take appropriate action, up to and including termination."

If the answer is found to be yes, begin the formal investigation. (More on this in a moment.)

Claim substantiated? If the answer is no, we will once again bring the parties together to resolve the claim. If the answer is yes, we take appropriate action.

The point of this simple example is to illustrate that at each stop along the chart, the questions asked and the information gathered will point the investigator in a specific direction.
This is a key:

> *Follow the flow of the information and let it take you in a logical direction*

You will find this to be true in most cases. Once the process begins, it will assume a life of its own. All you have to do is be open to it and remember the five rules outlined in Chapter Three.

THE INVESTIGATION PROCESS

The process begins with the rights of the charging party and the alleged harasser, which are summarized in the table that follows.

Rights of Both Parties After a Complaint Is Filed
The Charging Party
• Expedited review
• Investigation of the complaint
• Interview of witnesses or those having knowledge of the alleged event
• No retaliation for filing the complaint
• Privacy concerning the event and its outcome
The Accused
• Expedited review
• To have his or her day in court
• No predetermination of guilt
• Interview of witnesses or those having knowledge of the alleged event
• Privacy concerning the event and its outcome
Both Parties Have a Right to a Confidential Investigation

Notice that the rights are essentially the same. The accused has a right to the presumption of innocence while the charging party has a right to an expedited review. Both parties retain the right of privacy and a total right to a confidential investigation. In effect, we start on neutral ground *with both parties.*

The Process: Remember the Steps

The process used should be consistently applied from one case to another. Just make sure that the investigation will get at all the facts and lead to a well-thought-out and documentable conclusion. Here is a summary of the process that uses the word **INVESTIGATE** for easy recall.

The Investigative Process

- **I**dentify and interview the parties involved
- **N**otify each interviewee of a time for the interview
- **V**olatile, emotional situations may result
- **E**xamine all of the data thoroughly
- **S**trive to be fair and impartial
- **T**ake your time
- **I**nspect your notes a final time
- **G**ive your conclusions
- **A**lways consult before taking action
- **T**ake action
- **E**valuate and follow up

Each step will require additional actions and considerations.

(1) Identify and interview the parties involved.
- The charging party and the alleged harasser will each supply an initial set of names of persons they feel will have knowledge of the event. This is the "minimum" list for the investigation.
- If other names are offered, you will plan to interview them as well.

(2) Notify each interviewee of a time for the interview.

- Do so face to face and let them know why you are interviewing them. This gives them time to really think about what they know, and it is an important opportunity to spell out your expectations concerning confidentiality.
- There should be two people assigned to interview each person. Both must take notes as a double check of the information heard or offered.

(3) Volatile emotional situations may result.

- Prepare for the worst. Develop an action plan to deal with the potential for anger (i.e., have the employee paraphrase in order to cool them down, or dismiss until the next day; each can be effective in dealing with anger).

(4) Examine all of the data thoroughly.

- The two investigators will prepare their notes separately to help eliminate bias and allow the investigators to be as objective as possible. Differing recollections must be reconciled through additional interviews.
- Remember: your notes are subject to the legal process of discovery. They must be an accurate reflection of what you found in the interview process.

(5) Strive to be fair and impartial.
- Never take sides. Let the information lead you to a decision.
- Continually challenge yourself by asking: "If a jury heard this information, what would the members think?"

(6) Take your time.
- Do not be rushed to a conclusion. If the information says to re-interview anyone, do it. If the information takes you in a different direction, go there. Don't quit until the information is exhausted. Remember that jobs are at stake and legal action is a potential.

(7) Inspect your notes a final time.
- Both investigators will compare their notes a final time to make certain that they reached an impartial decision.

(8) Give your conclusions.
- Give your reports to the individuals who will make a decision on what to do about the case. This usually includes the Human Resources department and the respective department head.

- Keep it impartial. The investigators' tasks at this point are to present the facts and to explain the reasons for their conclusions. The investigators should not attempt to influence those hearing the information and the conclusion. The finding must speak for itself. If it does not, it may be weak. This is another checks-and-balances piece for the process.

(9) Always consult before taking action.
- If the action you are about to take includes termination, review the situation with the company's legal representative.
- If your discipline process requires a review process of some kind, make sure that you review it as outlined in the policy (i.e., reviews by plant manager, HR, etc.).

(10) Take action.
- Make sure that the action you are taking is consistent and appropriate for the behavior involved and consistent with your disciplinary procedure.

(11) Evaluate and follow up.
- The charging party and the alleged harasser are the only ones who will hear the decision of the investigation. The rule of confidentiality is explicitly followed, unless an individual has a clear *need to know*.

- The investigative team and those who review the data should challenge the process by asking themselves: "Were we fair and impartial, based on the evidence? Could we have conducted this investigation differently? Did we do the right thing?" If the answer is not *yes, no, yes*, your interview methods may need adjustment. Being overly critical of yourself will increase your objectivity, and that's what you should strive to achieve.

TERMINATION

Most organizations have a progressively scaled discipline process that has several phases before termination. Something like this:

- Verbal   A first meeting to discuss issues

- Written   A second meeting/opportunity to discuss and resolve continuing issues

- Final   A final meeting/opportunity to discuss and resolve continuing issues

- Discharge

If the employee refuses to change his or her problematic behavior, he or she is "walked" through the process.

There are some situations in which the requirement for progressive discipline is waived. Sexual harassment is one of those issues. It is a violation where termination is a *possibility* on a *first violation*. It is a behavior most juries will not tolerate, particularly if it is blatant. But should you terminate? This is always a difficult decision. Your decision however, will be easier to make and to justify if you include the following language in your policy and procedures manual and handbook, and post it on all bulletin boards:

> *Sexual harassment is a violation of company policy. One of our company's basic tenets is to provide a workplace free from such activity. Anyone found to be in violation of this policy will be subject to disciplinary action up to and including termination.*

This strong language lets everyone know the company considers harassment *serious*. It places everyone on notice. But before you terminate:

- Investigate.
- Get decision-makers involved.
- Follow the guidelines outlined in your discipline process.

I cannot overemphasize the need to investigate. In the California case, *Cotran v. Rollins Hudig Hall International, Inc.*, the court ruled that employers have the ability to terminate employees based upon a good faith belief that misconduct occurred. According to the decision, a good faith conclusion can be defined as "a reasoned conclusion . . . supported by substantial evidence *gathered through an adequate investigation* that includes notice of the claimed misconduct *and a chance for the employee to respond.*"

The lesson from this decision is this:

The Employer must:
❏ Develop a process to investigate all alleged incidents of harassment.
❏ Investigate all alleged incidents of harassment.
❏ Make sure the facts fit a reasoned conclusion.
❏ Make sure that the investigation includes an opportunity for the alleged harasser to respond to the claims made against him or her.

Here is the ultimate litmus test for any investigation. When it is concluded, ask yourself and others assigned to investigate this question: *If this information were ever subjected to third-party review, would those reviewing it come to the same conclusion?* If your answer is no, do *not* terminate until you are totally comfortable in answering yes.

The investigation process introduced in this chapter is not an option. It is imperative that you follow it *precisely.*

DOCUMENTING THE FINDINGS

Harassment is unique in that termination can result from such activity the first time it happens. Because notes are subject to the legal process of discovery, it is essential that the company details every step of the internal investigation. The company must be comfortable supporting a "no fault" finding or a finding of "guilty." The discovery process requires you to answer the following questions:

1. When did the company learn of the harassment?
2. When did the company begin its investigation?
3. Where did it happen?
4. Who was interviewed?
5. Why was he or she interviewed?
6. Who did the interviewing?
7. What was discovered?
8. Were both the charging party and the alleged harasser interviewed?

Each of these questions is essential to demonstate due process (procedural consistency). But equally important is the documentation you give to the charging party and the alleged harasser. It should "mirror" the above questions and look something like this:

Sample letter to support a finding of guilty

Mr. John Doe:

On April 4, it was brought to my attention that you were accused of engaging in inappropriate activity and conduct. As a result, the company began an immediate investigation into the alleged event. Our investigation included interviews with the charging party and with you, in order to gather all of the information available to help in our investigation and subsequent decision concerning your continued employment. Our investigatory process also included interviewing witnesses identified by you and the charging party.

As a result of our investigation, we have concluded that the conduct in question was inappropriate, per our harassment prevention policy, and we find it necessary to terminate your employment. I have attached the policy for your review and information. The policy was given to you when you were hired and is posted throughout the facility. As you can discern, harassment is not tolerated by our company and it is a terminable offense.

This simple letter accomplishes a number of important objectives if the company finds itself involved in some kind of legal action and must defend its position.

1. It states the day the company learned of the alleged harassment.
2. It states that the company took immediate action.
3. It confirms that the alleged harasser was given a chance to respond.
4. It shows that a process was established and used.
5. It reinforces the company's position (the policy is attached to the letter given the accused).
6. It demonstrated prior notification of the possible actions the company could take when it was posted on bulletin boards.
7. It details the fact that the employee knew of the policy because it was given at hire or at a training program.

The harasser at this point may wish to know who was interviewed. The names should not be given to the person. This is a confidential matter and the rights of the witnesses are equally protected.

Once you have taken the action to terminate, the charging party must be informed of the decision.

ACTIONS TO SUPPORT A FINDING OF *NOT GUILTY*

When the information gathered does not support the allegations, it is suggested that you meet with each party separately to inform them of the findings. (You will bring them together later to work out their differences and feelings.) The alleged harasser may want something in writing from you confirming your findings. This is a natural reaction to something as serious as harassment. Suggested wording will look something like this:

> Mr. John Doe:
>
> We have completed our investigation concerning your alleged harassment. The process involved interviewing a number of individuals supplied by you and the charging party. As a result, it is our reasoned conclusion that there is a misunderstanding of the actions (or events) of March 3 and that your behavior was misinterpreted. We appreciate your help in bringing this matter to resolution.

Or, in the case of questionable activity:

> We have completed our investigation concerning your alleged harassment. The process involved interviewing a number of individuals recommended by you and the charging party. As a result, it is our

> reasoned conclusion that while your behavior was inappropriate [**define here (e.g., a single flirtatious episode)**], it was not harassment because you ceased the activity when instructed to do so by the charging party. We must caution you, however, to consider the feelings of others before you take such latitude again. Any other occurrence of the same behavior can subject you to discipline up to and including termination.

After notifying both parties of your decision not to terminate, I recommended that you arrange for someone skilled in conflict resolution to meet with both parties. This person should discuss the nature of the complaint and allow the employees to talk about how each felt as a result of the ensuing action. This is an important step to diffuse any underlying hostility and help create a new working relationship.

Our ultimate goal is not to investigate harassment, but to prevent it. Let's look at some causes and ways to stop this activity before it starts.

5
STOPPING HARASSMENT

Employers and employees alike have more to concern themselves with than worrying about harassment. It should be a non-existent workplace issue, given that the law is unmistakably clear. So, why does it exist? I believe there are four reasons:

(1) Accidents do happen.
- Someone said something inadvertently off-color and it was overheard by an individual who took offense.
- Someone didn't know their audience and spoke "out of order."

(2) Messages are taken out of context.
- What the person said versus what the person heard are two different things.

(3) Sexuality is alive and well in the workplace.
- And the law will never prevent the natural attraction inherent in people.

(4) Some people will push the envelope.
- For whatever reason, he or she doesn't seem to understand that harassment is against the law.

This is quite a list. At first glance, an initial thought might be, "If this is true, how do I stop it?" There are three ways to approach the issue of harassment prevention:

Three ways to control harassment
1. Educate
2. Communicate
3. Eliminate

EDUCATION

Harassment awareness training should be conducted at least every other year. All new employees should be required to attend the training program within three months of being hired and be given a copy of your policy when they accept the position. The company's policy on workplace harassment should be distributed at these training sessions and posted for all to see. The cafeteria or other break areas are mandatory areas for posting. A book such as this one should be distributed to employees or used to develop a training seminar. At a minimum, the seminar must cover:

1. The company policy
2. The definitions of harassment
3. The investigation procedure
4. The penalties associated with violation of the policy
5. How to report suspected harassment
6. Suggested employee response to harassing situations (e.g. tell the offender to stop)

COMMUNICATION

Communication is more than what you write or say to educate your employees about policy. It also encompasses how individuals verbalize their discomfort in a harassing situation.

Two questions must be answered. What do I do if I feel I have been harassed? What if my direct approach doesn't work?

The first approach involves telling the person to stop the activity in question. As I said earlier, do not expect change until you have set the expectation for it. Basic reinforcement theory states that if you want to decrease the likelihood of something reoccurring, extinguish it.

> *To decrease the likelihood of reoccurring behavior, extinguish it through verbalization.*

One can extinguish offensive behavior by voicing displeasure. The message will be succinct and to the point and will emphasize that the person's activity is *unwelcome* and *unwanted*. The comments will reflect the nature of the offending conduct and the expectations for change. Something like this:

"I would like to keep our working relationship strictly professional. I do not wish to see you outside of our workplace."

Or

"I find your telling racial jokes very offensive. Please do not tell them in my presence again."

Or

"Your constant staring at me is very rude. Please do not stare at me anymore."

If this doesn't work, the person is left with little choice but to report it to someone in authority. A management person or someone in human resources is a logical choice. No matter who the company designates to hear complaints, make sure the individual is properly trained to deal with them.

Conduct Considerations

A good point to get across in any training seminar is how one would feel if he or she were harassed. When it hits home, it becomes a real issue. Here is another suggested communication format:

The 3 A's of Conduct

(1) **A**ge of the golden rule
   - Do unto others.
   - What if it happened to a family member or someone you care for? How would you feel?

(2) **A**void behavior that degrades, abuses, shows disrespect, demeans, denigrates others, etc.
   - Think before you speak.
   - Think before you act.

(3) **A**udience specifics must be kept in mind at all times.
   - Know your audience but think before you speak.

We can summarize the basic intent of communications with the following chart and this statement:

> *Inform to reform*

**Communicate Intent to Prevent
and Take Action Against Harassment**

Inform to Reform

The Company will...   notify employees with written materials and through training.

The Employee will...   notify the offender that he or she must cease any unwanted and unwelcome behaviors.

In each example, ownership in the process becomes key. The company assumes responsibility in the first example; the employee takes responsibility in the second.

The company accomplishes its task in three ways: it conducts recurrent training on the subject matter of harassment; it posts its policy for all to see; and it makes sure the policy is part of any employee handbooks and manuals.

The employee accomplishes his or her task by immediately informing any transgressor of unwanted or unwelcome behaviors to immediately cease such behavior in his or her presence.

TERMINATION

Unfortunately, some will never get it and your only option for this type of behavior will be to remove the offender through termination. As I mentioned at the very beginning of this book, in our litigious society termination is always a risk. In this workplace issue, however, if you have done your homework and investigated and documented the facts, it is an acceptable, albeit calculated, risk. If you terminate, make sure you review your reasons and facts with those who approve terminations, as identified in Chapter Three.

Encourage Sensitivity

The bottom line to any effective training program on harassment prevention is sensitivity. That is, each person must understand the issue and feel the discomfort of someone experiencing harassment. Here is an exercise that will help. It is called "Perspectives: Cease and Desist."

Perspectives: Cease and Desist		
	Men	Women
Cease	1.	1.
	2.	2.
	3.	3.

Directions: Divide the group by gender. Ask each group to come up with three things they need to Cease and Desist from the perspective of the other group. As an example, the men might list:

1. **Cease**—telling offensive jokes in the presence of women.

   or

2. **Cease**—the use of sexual innuendo or slang in the work environment.

The women might list:

1. **Cease**—stereotyping all men as potential harassers.

   or

2. **Cease**—my avoidance behaviors for fear of sending the wrong signals.

This exercise requires a trained facilitator, one who knows how to deal with both positive and negative feedback, and knows how to turn the latter into a greater sense of understanding of individual differences.

6
PERSONAL COMMITMENT TO PREVENTING HARASSMENT

If you are reading this book or using it to design a training seminar, you understand the importance of a company's commitment to harassment prevention. Here is your opportunity to detail each individual's action plan. If used in a training seminar, each participant should be encouraged to complete it.

> I understand that harassment is not tolerated by my company and I am personally committed to eliminating it as a workplace issue. I am prepared to do the following:
>
> * _____
>
> * _____
>
> * _____
>
> * _____
>
> I will follow up with (insert name) in two months to discuss my progress in meeting my objectives.
>
> Name: _____

You can tie this easily into the previous exercise. Each "bullet" could be filled from the "cease" definitions.

YOUR HARASSMENT POLICY

Throughout the book I have emphasized the importance of a policy on harassment prevention. I suggest that you post your policy and include it in the employee handbook. Here is one you may wish to use. You can change the wording to fit your organization's culture.

SAMPLE POLICY
OUR COMMITMENT
XYZ company is committed to providing a workplace where all employees have the opportunity to contribute to its success. Our goal is to create an environment that will provide respect for the individual and freedom from harassment.
This policy summarizes our philosophy prohibiting workplace harassment. As an employee you should familiarize yourself with and adhere to these policies and procedures. If you have any questions or concerns about this issue, please speak with your supervisor or a representative from Human Resources. They are always available to hear you and assist you.

(continued)

Our success in stopping harassment is determined by you and your commitment. By fostering respect and dignity for each other, we can ensure that all employees have the opportunity to reach their maximum potential at XYZ.

WHAT IS WORKPLACE HARASSMENT?

Workplace harassment is any unwelcome or unwanted conduct based on an individual's race, sex, ethnic or national origin, age, religion, disability, sexual preference, or other personal characteristic.

WHAT IS SEXUAL HARASSMENT?

Sexual harassment is a form of sex discrimination also involving unwanted or unwelcome conduct. Harassing activity can be male to female, female to male, or involve the same sex. Harassment in any form, whether defined as verbal, non-verbal, physical advance, request for sexual favors, or other conduct of a sexual nature affecting an individual's work environment, will not be tolerated.

(continued)

Examples:

Verbal harassment includes sexual innuendo and other suggestive comments; racial or ethnic slurs; humor and jokes about sex, race, age, religion, disability, sexual orientation, or gender-specific traits; sexual advances or propositions; insults or threats.

Non-Verbal harassment includes leering; whistling; suggestive or insulting looks, sounds, gestures, pictures, cartoons, or calendars; or offensive or derogatory written materials.

Physical harassment is the intentional touching of the body (e.g., brushing, patting, pinching); kissing; inappropriate display of the body; coerced acts of a sexual nature; or exclusionary or demeaning actions or activities based on age, ethnicity, sex, or race.

CONDUCT CONSIDERATIONS

The company expects you to make sure your conduct is appropriate at all times. You should *avoid* behavior that degrades, abuses, or shows disrespect to any individual. *Recognize* that the same remarks acceptable to some people may be embarrassing or unwanted by others.

(continued)

STOPPING HARASSMENT

The most effective way to put an end to inappropriate behavior is to tell the person to stop. Be direct so that the person knows the seriousness of your message. If the direct approach doesn't work, report the situation to your manager or to Human Resources.

COMPANY RESPONSE TO HARASSMENT

The company will investigate all alleged charges of harassment. Any person found to be in violation will be subject to disciplinary action up to and including termination. The charging party will be informed of the action taken against the offender. Retaliation against anyone seeking redress for harassment will not be tolerated.

REPORTING HARASSMENT

If you feel you have been harassed, you are free to discuss the issue with any member of management. The Human Resources department staff is also available to hear your complaint. Any report of harassment will be investigated immediately. The charging party will be informed of the decision reached after a thorough investigation.

Exercise: Find the Common Ground

Here is a good exercise that makes an important point: if we all search long enough, we can find something in common. That "something" is the start of understanding and open communication.

The instructor will stand on one side of the room with all class participants standing on the other side of the room facing the instructor. The instructor will make a series of statements. Each time someone agrees with the instructor, they move to the instructor's side of the room. Here are some examples:

(1) Join me if your favorite color is red.
(2) Join me if your favorite color is blue.
(3) Join me if you like Motown music.
(4) Join me if you want to retire before the age of sixty.
(5) Join me if you do not know how to swim.
(6) Join me if you think there was a conspiracy to kill JFK and Martin Luther King.
(7) Join me if you think cartoons are too violent.

You can add statements as you see fit.

Eventually, everyone will join the instructor. Ask the participants to share what they have learned from this exercise.

GETTING TO KNOW YOU

Here is an exercise I call "Getting to Know You." It is a good icebreaker at the very beginning of a seminar on harassment prevention. It forces attendees to mix and get to know something about one another. It also points out cultural differences essential in this class and to our understanding of our own biases.

Directions: *Find someone who can answer the questions in the boxes. Have them initial the box if it applies to them.*		
Has Read the Company's Harassment Policy ☐	Can Define Diversity ☐	Knows What the Pygmalion Effect Means ☐
Can Define Non-Verbal Harassment ☐	Has Experienced Stereotyping ☐	Knows What Quid Pro Quo Means ☐
Is a Veteran ☐	Has Experienced Harassment ☐	Can Define Workforce 2000 ☐
Can Define Perception vs. Reality ☐	Dislikes the Chicago Bulls ☐	Is in a Protected Class ☐

Workforce 2000: A study concluding that more minorities and females will be in the workforce than white males by the year 2000. (By the Hudson Institute)

Quid Pro Quo: Something for something.

Perception vs. Reality: There is no difference. Perception is a person's reality.

Protected Class: Can be a female, over 40, Vietnam-era veteran, a person of color, etc.

Pygmalion: If you think you can do something . . . you can.

THE FIVE A'S OF UNDERSTANDING

I introduced this concept at the beginning of the book. Its purpose is to celebrate those value-added differences we all bring into the workplace and to clarify the company's expectations. Here are suggestions as to how to use them:

1. **A**ppreciate and celebrate workforce diversity.
2. **A**dvance the understanding of different cultures and ideologies.

You can do this by:

- Establishing cultural awareness days. Designate a group (e.g., African American, Hispanic, Asian, Native American) to develop written informational pieces that detail the history of the culture, heroes within the culture (e.g., Martin Luther King), the significance of holidays within the culture (Ramadan), etc. A good place to display the works is in the company cafeteria.

3. **A**lways tune in to messages sent to you.

   - Establish *and use* an open-door policy at all levels of the organization. Break down barriers created by position. Develop and use a reporting procedure for complaints of any nature.

   - Establish a suggestion box.

   - Establish a central telephone number for individuals to call if they have questions or suggestions.

   - Establish an e-mail address for questions or suggestions.

4. **A**nnounce at every opportunity your commitment to create a professional work environment free of unacceptable behaviors.

   - Discuss your philosophy at meetings and other formal work gatherings.

- Publish your statements in employee handbooks, in your policy and procedures manual, and in annual reports.

5. **A**lign your policies and procedures to reflect your attitude and statements.

- Establish a committee to continually review company practices and policies to make sure they reflect and support your statements. For example, does your harassment policy include statements on non-tolerance, penalties for non-compliance, definitions, etc.?

YOUR QUESTIONS & ANSWERS

All employees should have an idea about what to do if they feel they have been harassed. Here is something to consider for your policy manual; it is also suitable for posting on bulletin boards and for use in any harassment training seminar.

What You Should Know

Q. There seem to be so many definitions for harassment. How do I know if I have been harassed, with all of these definitions?

A. If something has made you feel uncomfortable, tell your supervisor or report it to someone in the Human Resources department. This not only surfaces the issue so we can deal with it, but it also allows for prompt resolution if there is an issue.

Q. Is there a one best way to stop harassment?

A. Yes. Tell the person to stop. Explain that his or her behavior is unacceptable to you. If this does not work, report the activity to your supervisor or to Human Resources.

Q. How do I report it?

A. Our procedure is as follows:
   - ❑ Report the incident to your supervisor. If this person is unavailable, report to his or her supervisor.
   - ❑ Report the incident to Human Resources if the alleged harasser is your supervisor or if you are uncomfortable going to him or her.
   - ❑ Report the incident to anyone serving in a supervisory capacity, if you are comfortable with that person.

Q. What actions can I expect the company to take concerning my report?

A. The company is obligated by law to investigate your complaint. We will thoroughly and immediately look into the matter.

Q. Will I be informed of any action taken against the person harassing me?

A. Yes. Both you and the charging party will be informed.

Q. What if I don't want the harasser terminated?

A. The company will consider your feelings, but we will determine the correct course of action based on the nature of the event and its impact on you, your co-workers, and the company.

Q. Is it okay to date co-workers, given the issue of harassment?

A. The company does not want to be to intrusive into the private lives of its employees, but dating co-workers is discouraged and if you do date, you must keep your working relationship strictly professional. We discourage dating because if the relationship ends, it can be a problem later on.

Q. Can I file my complaint outside of the company?

A. Yes. Agencies such as the Equal Employment Opportunity Commission (EEOC) are available to hear your complaint. However, we would like the chance to deal with the issue first. Oftentimes we can remedy most internal problems.

Q. What if a co-worker is harassed? Should I report it?

A. What *you* might consider as harassment another might not. Ask the co-worker to come forward if they have any concerns. We want to resolve any questionable issues as early as possible.

Q. What if I report harassment and I am made to feel uncomfortable as a result?

A. Anyone who retaliates against you for filing a charge of harassment is subject to discipline up to and including termination. If you feel you are experiencing retaliation, report it to your supervisor immediately.

LET'S TAKE A TEST

Read the following case and answer the questions to determine your understanding of harassment issues.

John has been working with Mary for a couple of years now. They take lunches together and they have been seen after hours at a local pub. It is no secret that they have dated once or twice, but that is all. Mary has told her associates that she has no continuing interest in him, nor does she plan on allowing the relationship to go any further. John, on the other hand, thinks Mary is something special. He is sending her notes at work and calling her in the evenings. He is quick to point out at work how sexy she looks and has said so in front of others, much to Mary's embarrassment. Mary recently told John she wants to keep things on a professional level and that the notes and calls are no longer wanted. John just won't take no for an answer. The notes and calls keep coming. He thinks he can win her over with them.

Please answer the following questions:

(1) Is dating a co-worker harassment?
             Yes   No
(2) Does sending notes at work constitute harassment?
             Yes   No
(3) Does calling Mary after hours constitute harassment?
             Yes   No
(4) Is telling Mary she is sexy in front of others harassment?
             Yes   No
(5) At what point did John cross the line into activity that constitutes harassment?
             Yes   No

Let's examine each question.

Is dating a co-worker harassment?

No, but this is a good opportunity to show that dating is an activity that should be discouraged. The differing perceptions of John and Mary present an issue where the company may be at risk. At a minimum, it must look into Mary's complaint even though the relationship was (at one time) consensual.

Does sending notes at work constitute harassment?

Where two parties welcome the notes, the answer is no. In this case, however, Mary has told John she wants them to stop. They are now unwanted and unwelcome.

Does calling Mary after hours constitute harassment?

This is the same as the previous question. If the parties welcome the activity, it is not harassment. In this case, it would constitute harassment, as Mary has told John to stop.

Is telling Mary she is sexy harassment?

Even if Mary welcomed this comment, it could be offensive to others who demand a professional working environment. Remember, it is not just those who actually experience the harassment. Harassment can include those who see it or hear it and are offended by it.

At what point did John cross the line into activity that constitutes harassment?

From Mary's perspective, it became unwanted and unwelcome activity when she told John to stop. A co-worker could have taken offense sooner as a result of John's comments, notes, and calls at work.

PROGRAM EVALUATION FORM

If you decide to use this book to develop a training program, here is a form to administer at the end of the session. It will help you get feedback on the program's effectiveness and help you redesign it if necessary.

Date: _____
Trainer Name(s): _____

How effective was this program in providing you with a working knowledge of workplace harassment?
- Very Effective
- Effective
- Marginally Effective
- No Change

How effective was this program in helping you examine your own behaviors, attitudes, and biases, and how you can change?
- Very Effective
- Effective
- Marginally Effective
- No change

What were the most valuable learning experiences for you?
_____
_____

What were the least valuable learning experiences for you?
_____
_____

Is there anything you would like to see added to the program?
_____
_____

In Summary
❑ Develop your policy: disseminate and post it in a highly visible area
❑ Train everyone on harassment, not just supervisors: annual review is recommended
❑ Distribute your harassment policy and train all new hires within the first week of hire
❑ Give vendors, temporary employees, contractors and consultants your policy prior to the commencement of work or site visitation
❑ Immediately investigate all claims of harassment
❑ Encourage open door to report instances of suspected harassment
❑ Follow your rules
❑ Consult with your legal counsel prior to any harassment related disciplinary action
❑ Document, Document, Document
Harassment Prevention Musts

CONCLUSION

Every employer *must* develop a policy concerning workplace harassment; distribute that policy to employees; follow it implicitly; and provide regular training on the subject of harassment. These actions will not only earn the respect of your employees, they will provide the company with some protection should legal action be taken. ***Two final items:*** If you receive a harassment complaint, act on it immediately. I've seen too many employers drag their feet to the point where the charging party thinks nothing is being done. The charging party then takes his or her complaint elsewhere for action. *Do not allow this to happen.* Try to solve your problems internally, and do not let them escalate. And, if something doesn't feel right, don't do it. If you are about to say something and you have a momentary flash that tells you not to say it, don't say it. Be proactive in your efforts to curb harassment.

I hope this *Manager's Pocket Guide to Preventing Sexual Harassment* helps you better understand this important issue and provides you with an impetus for change.

Terry Fitzwater

INDEX

ABOUT THE AUTHOR

TERRY L. FITZWATER is managing partner of Fitzwater Leadership Consulting, which specializes in employee relations and organization development. He spent nearly two decades with a Fortune 100 company as Vice President of Human Resources—West. Terry is a frequent speaker on current employee relations and can provide further information on harassment and other seminar topics. He can be reached at (916) 791-7938 or (916) 791-0692. His e-mail address is tfitzh2o@quiknet.com.

Endorsement

This guide is easy to understand and provides tools and suggestions to identify and deal with harassment awareness and prevention. We have used the materials to teach our employees on this critical business issue and the feedback was excellent. I highly recommend this book.

Leslie Lundberg
VP of Human Resources
TIMET
Denver, CO